My Note for You:

FOR LEA.
THANK YOU FOR "ZU DIR" - MY INSPIRATION.

SISTERLY
Published by LHC Publishing 2021

Printed in the USA.

All inquiries should be directed to
www.LHCpublishing.com

ISBN-13: 978-1-952517-07-5 Paperback
ISBN-13: 978-1-952517-06-8 Hardcover

Life's Biggest Moments

SISTERLY

To my Best Friend

WRITTEN BY
EEVI JONES

My Sweet Sister:

If I had to list all the things that I love,
'bout you, my sister, my friend,
this is what I'd share,
with every word felt and meant.

You hold my hand, you've got my back
through thick and thin, each day.
You wipe away my big ol' tears,
when times are tough and gray.

You pick me up, and dust me off;
take care of my scraped knees,
when after my attempts to soar,
I stumble, fall, or freeze.

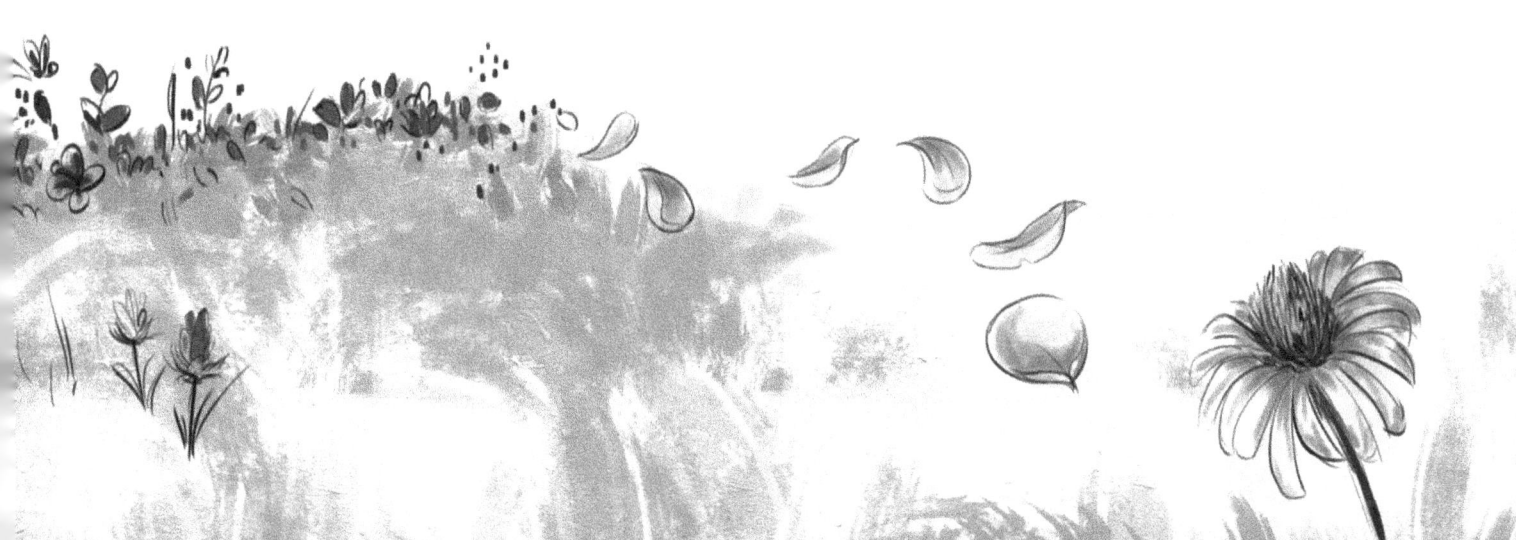

You're the wind inside my sail,
my biggest fan of all.
Lifting and supporting me,
you catch me when I fall.

When wings are bent, need mending
after an unsuccessful try,
you're the one that helps me
remember how to fly.

With you, I can be fully me;
myself – all raw and true.
Without a filter, plain, with flaws,
I can count on you.

When dreams pop like a bubble,
when hope turns into none,
you remind me steadfastly,
that my fierce has only just begun.

When the happy overtakes my heart,
when bliss grows wide and tall,
when joy no longer stays contained,
you're the first one I would call.

When I've been stripped of everything,
lost ways, all hope, unfree;
in need of roof and shelter,
you are there for me.

When ashamed, embarrassed, flustered,
because of mistakes made and done,
you help me find solutions
where I thought there would be none.

Late night talks til mornings,
mornings turning into brunch.
A call meant as a quick hello,
now lasting way past lunch.

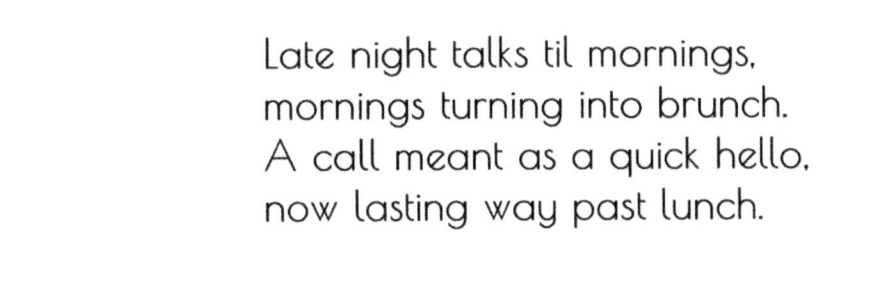

You see through my smiles,
you push past my veils.
You break through my walls,
can tell truth from my tales.

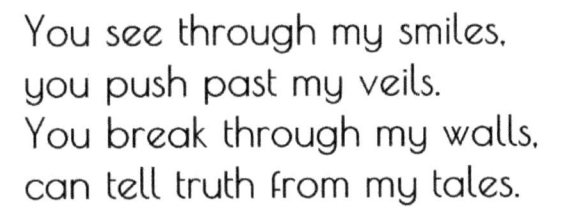

I don't have to say it with words,
because you already know.
While things around me shift and change,
you've become my constant ages ago.

No matter what will be, what is, or what was;
you know me, my ticks, and my faults.
Together we're silly and wacky and nuts,
while others have long joined the world of adults.

You are my mirror,
when I don't remember who I am.
You show me the way,
when lost in glitter and false glam.

You are my quiet in the noise of this world;
my sea, my ocean, my deep.
You are my harbor and haven
where my truth I can fearlessly speak.

My sister, whether by blood or by heart.
My friend and ally for life.
You push me to grow and to bloom;
to reach for the stars; to thrive.

For you, I'd walk to the end of this world,
in heels, through storms and through droughts.
With a million and one against your word,
I'd believe YOU, without any doubts.

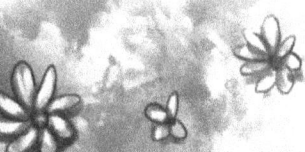

There's just one person I trust fully,
without exception, through and through.
No holding back, no hesitation.
And that person - it is you!

Our memories made and shared
I'll treasure til the end.
Lovingly and sisterly,
for YOU are my BEST friend.

ABOUT THE AUTHOR

Writing under a number of pen names, Eevi Jones is a USA Today & WSJ bestselling and award-winning author and ghostwriter of children's books.

Born in former East Germany to a German mother and a Vietnamese father, Eevi loves to infuse her children's books with racial diversity. Always drawing inspiration from her own two children, she writes about unique interests and aspires to find fun and exciting ways to have kids discover and learn about the magnificent marvels this world has to offer.

Eevi has been featured in Forbes, Scary Mommy, Business Insider, Huffington Post, Exceptional Parent Magazine, and more.

She can be found online at www.BravingTheWorldBooks.com.

A WORD BY THE AUTHOR

Whether by blood or by heart, your sweet sister is your ally for life. I hope that with this book you come to see how very precious you are to each other, and what magical moments and memories you have forged and created with one another. How lucky are we to have such a beautiful, magnificent soul in our lives?

If you enjoyed this book, it would mean the world to me if you would take a short minute to leave a heartfelt review. Thank you.

OTHER WORKS BY THIS AUTHOR

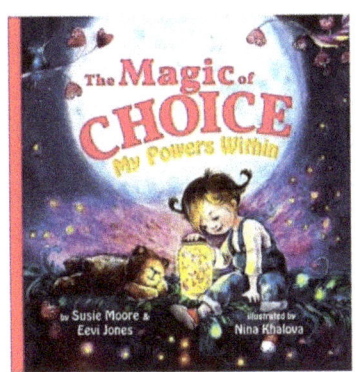

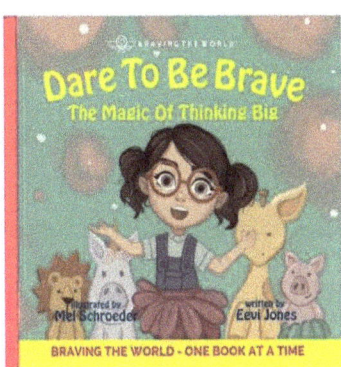

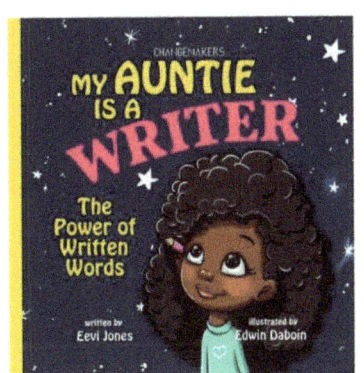

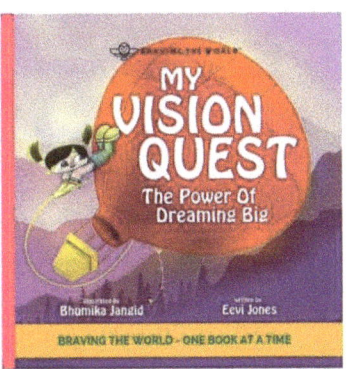

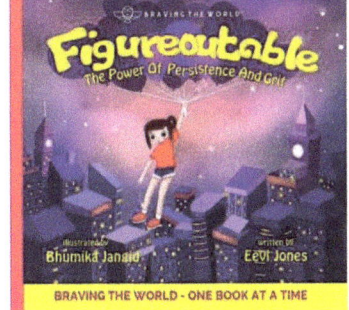

... AND MANY MORE

www.ingramcontent.com/pod-product-compliance
Lightning Source LLC
LaVergne TN
LVHW070121100526
838202LV00011B/328